ANNEXATION OF SANTO DOMINGO.

SPEECH

OF

HON. JUSTIN S. MORRILL,

OF VERMONT,

DELIVERED

IN THE SENATE OF THE UNITED STATES,

APRIL 7, 1871.

WASHINGTON:
F. & J. RIVES & GEO. A. BAILEY,
REPORTERS AND PRINTERS OF THE DEBATES OF CONGRESS.
1871.

ANNEXATION OF SANTO DOMINGO.

Mr. MORRILL, of Vermont. Mr. President, let me say in the outset that the message from the President, accompanying the report of the commissioners, has my cordial approval. If a partisan press has heretofore assailed his character, that, in the face of the report, will be no longer possible. The President wisely remits the question to the voice of the people, and stands, as at his inauguration, with no policy to enforce against their wishes. This I regard as an end of a vexed question; and I should not have trespassed upon the patience of the Senate only that I think it just and fair that some of the reasons for regarding the annexation of Santo Domingo with disfavor should be allowed to have utterance at the same time with the dissemination of a report which is likely to attract more or less the attention of the country.

Mr. President, differing as I do from the President as to his Santo Domingo policy, it is only just to say in the outset that I have ever freely accorded to him the credit of being actuated by the purest motives in whatever he has done to promote the swift accomplishment of annexation. In his methods he may have committed errors, but his intentions, I feel confident, will bear the scrutiny of the final Judge of all men. Let those who have done truer and braver work for their country, if any such there be, assail President Grant, but as for me I hold no title to give point to any sentence with the purpose of inflicting a stab upon his reputation. All parts of his late annual message were able—most of it exceedingly satisfactory to the country—but there was no part of it more elaborate than that touching Santo Domingo. It is a subject deserving serious examination, and I wish an answer might be made in terms as terse and of equal clearness as those employed in the message; but it is my purpose to touch upon only a few of the points there and elsewhere so strongly urged. In doing this, however, I shall be frank and earnest. Less than this would neither be truthful to the State I in part represent nor respectful to the Senate.

The report of the commissioners may speak well of the climate because, in five weeks, it never hurt them; favorably of the soil because it really produces bananas and pine-apples, never seen in Ohio, New York, or Massachusetts; slightingly of the iron, copper, and gold mines, as they had annihilated "distance," the only thing that "lends enchantment to the view," and the inhabitants may not have been aware that they were expected to produce anything valuable of this sort; despondingly of finding coal at Samana, where there is only a poor show of lignite; but the report will be well sprinkled with salt—Syracuse must look after its saltness—and yet it will be found neither more exhaustive nor reliable than a large number of works from the hands of impartial travelers who have heretofore visited the island and devoted far more time to the investigation of facts. Their report may be faithful as to what they saw, but it cannot supersede authorities of equal character and much larger opportunities, and will be chiefly valuable for vindicating, what needed no vindication, the personal integrity of the President and that of the gallant young officer charged with negotiating the defeated treaty.

ANNEXATION FINAL—DIVORCE FOREVER IMPOSSIBLE.

A treaty, or joint resolution, of annexation once made and adopted must be final and irrevocable. However sad and long the train of evils succeeding, there is absolutely no remedy. Divorce is impossible. After the Missouri pours its muddy flood into the Mississippi, the Father of Waters never again recovers its original purity, but rolls down its whole course in a foul, discolored, and turbid condition, until, through a half dozen wide-gaping mouths, it disembogues into the great Gulf below. Let this West India stream of annexation but once pour its foul current into the history of the United States, and its polluted track will be visible for all coming time, or so long as the Union shall be preserved from the great gulf below.

The annual message of the President brought into one golden sheaf the heads of a large number of arguments in behalf of Santo Domingo annexation, strong enough to stand while closely huddled together, but doomed to bend and fall one after another when standing alone and examined separately and apart, or when the rhetorical band holding them so snugly together has been once broken. The task of dealing with the whole of these state-paper suggestions would be an inviting one if assertions could be as briefly refuted as they can be briefly made. "There is but one God, and Mohammed is his prophet" is quickly and stoutly said; and while the first branch of the proposition receives universal assent, the last, though incredible, has to be refuted by the tedious processes of facts and arguments. I shall undertake to grapple with what may be considered the most material arguments in behalf of Dominican annexation, as well as a few of those requiring, it may be, some patience to consider, but patience only to refute.

A BULLY AMONG REPUBLICS NOT LOVED.

Our reputation among our sister republics in America is not wholly unblemished, nor is it, I fear, likely to grow brighter by the history of the Santo Domingo complications. Not that we have in our foreign relations always been in the wrong, but that we seem to have possessed a wonderful aptitude to get embroiled with weaker nationalities. All remember the circumstances of our troubles with Mexico, or of her troubles with us. We toré from her side the large State of Texas, and when she pouted about the extravagant boundary claimed we declared that war existed by her act, and fought bloody battles for three years to make her surrender and sell two or three more large States; but the wounds of poor Mexico have been bleeding ever since, and if we are looked upon with any favor, it is when in comparison with the French.

Then, in 1852, Greytown, the principal port of one of the republics of Central America, was bombarded and burned by a naval force of the United States, on the flimsy charge that its inhabitants had infringed the rights of the transit company. No reparation on our part has ever been made for this wanton and brutal exercise of power.

Soon after this commenced the career of the filibuster Walker; first in Sonora, Lower California, then in Nicaragua, where at last he was driven into Rivas, and, taking shelter on board the United States sloop-of-war St. Mary's, was brought to New Orleans, but only to receive sympathy, and not punishment, for his piratical achievements. Mr. Buchanan was loud in deprecating such crimes, but could find no authority for punishing the criminals. But when Walker, in 1860, struck at Honduras he was captured and met the fate he had so long deserved. His acts, nevertheless, ineffaceably stained the character of our country.

With Paraguay we had some difficulty, ten years ago or more, which caused us to send a formidable naval expedition there with threatening demands. Will she ever forget or forgive us?

Our attitude toward Cuba has frequently put our relations with Spain in jeopardy. Sometimes we propose to buy it at a great price, and sometimes our private citizens propose to take it by force at their own risk and expense.

In 1860 we withdrew our minister from Peru in consequence of the seizure of two American vessels which were illegally loaded with guano at an island from which the Peruvian Government did not permit it to be exported to foreign countries. Peru has paid no damages, and loves us little.

Only recently, while Brazil was at war with Paraguay, the passage of the American gunboat Wasp up the Paraguay to bring away the American minister, Mr. Washburn, was refused, and thereupon General Webb demanded an apology at a fixed time or he would close his diplomatic relations. The Brazilian Government sullenly complied, but our repeated offers thereafter to mediate in the war against Paraguay were steadily declined. Such kind offices, it is humiliating to admit, would be accepted by Brazil or almost any other American Government with more alacrity when tendered by European nations than if tendered by the United States.

This unpleasant recital might be continued, but is not this enough to require a little more circumspection on our part, and to see to it, while we submit to nothing wrong, that we do not carry ourselves like a bully among little nations?

The annexation of Santo Domingo, whether of spontaneous origin or nursed by the military, naval, and financial power of the United States, cannot fail to excite the jealousy and fear of all the American republics. The United States will be the great land-shark of the continent, whose friendship entices only to devour and whose anger can only be appeased by destruction. Our neighborhood, instead of being one of cordial sympathy and support, becomes one of apprehension and danger to all inferior independent Governments. May not any official, who can obtain nominal supremacy in the government of his people, count on the flag and the Treasury of the United States as an ally whenever he is ready to betray and sell his country? The American Republic should be the protector, the counselor, and guide of all her sister republics, and not a ravenous beast of prey.

If our natural growth prior to our late war excited the envy and distrust of the aristocracy of England and France, because, as they said, we were becoming too arrogant and aggressive, can we not be content therewith without seeking extraordinary accessions to our bulk, and such accessions, too, as will be far more likely to contribute to our downfall than to our up-building? The natural growth of a free country must be respected, be let alone, and will receive the universal admiration of freemen, but a forced or artificial growth is not only often circumvented, but nearly always a positive calamity.

ARE OUR PEOPLE NOW HOMOGENEOUS.

It is useless to disguise the fact that the people of a portion of our present territory have not become assimilated with the American people and American institutions, and the time when they will do so must be computed, not by years, but by generations. To say nothing of our lately acquired Siberia, commonly called Alaska, it must be conceded that Arizona, New Mexico, Utah, and that portion of Texas bordering upon Mexico are yet not only essentially un-American, but they have no overwhelming attachment to our form of government nor to the Anglo-Saxon race. Their first love was of a different complexion. If the strong arm of the United States should at any time become weak, it would receive no succor from these localities, (the conspicuous acquisitions of manifest destiny,) but their population would at any time, most likely, flock to the banner of any cocked-hat revolutionist. Their civilization is at variance and not in harmony with our own. Having little commerce and almost wholly destitute of educational institutions, they are making no advances in the arts or sciences, literature or politics, and are neither better nor worse than they were years ago. It is certainly a matter to be regretted that any portion of our Union should seem to lag in the rear of the highest type of civilization, but it must be a sorry consolation to them or to us to add to the Union still darker patches in order to give to the places indicated the conspicuous advantages of a contrast.

It is also to be apprehended that the late masters of the emancipated race in the southern States will make few sacrifices for the enlightenment of that race or do anything which will elevate the colored people above dependence. The unflinching policy of all the States lately in rebellion would seem to be to subordinate the black man, intellectually as well as politically, and to give him no means of support except in accordance with compacts to which he is not an equal party. Under a system like this millions of freedmen may continue to have their ancient ignorance fostered and perpetuated and the prospect of making them intelligent citizens, enjoying the protection of of our Government—if they can be said to enjoy it—and giving in return a full equivalent therefor, will not very speedily be realized. The result is that the master race, embittered by defeat in the recent conflict, studies political revenge for the future, and the freedman is to be kept in such poverty and ignorance as to make him of little value to himself and of still less to his country.

These may be unwelcome truths, but if their verity is undeniable, prudent statesmanship requires that we should not be deluded by the vain idea that the consequences may be avoided by denial or by silence. The risks of the future ought not to be multiplied, though all the ragged and fugitive kingdoms of the world should seek annexation to us and show an eagerness to undertake their part of the risk. There are but few of even the brightest spots on earth which under any circumstances would be acceptable to us, and none that should be urged by any appliances of the Treasury or Navy. We desire to retain the prestige of teaching nations by our example how to govern themselves, rather than to imperil our own existence by attempting to govern the incapables, whether near or remote, upon fat soils or lean. We cannot confer freedom upon any foreign people, much less upon a people who have not earned it, nor have the sense and energy to accept it. Freedom is the reward of merit, and not a subject of commerce or charity. At home we may make freemen of slaves or savages, but they will be so nominally only, requiring the protection of older freemen until they have been educated up to the point of appreciating their new privileges. Meanwhile they must be objects of solicitude, to some extent of weakness and of increased expenditure.

BAY OF SAMANA A COSTLY ELEPHANT.

One of the arguments in behalf of annexation is that we need the bay of Samana as a harbor for the protection of our commerce. Why do we need it? Certainly not for a coaling station unless we first carry coal there. Santo Domingo embraces the easternmost part of the island, far beyond St. Thomas, Cuba, and Jamaica, and almost entirely outside of the ordinary routes of commerce, with the Atlantic on one side and the Caribbean sea on the other. Even the steamships for Aspinwall pass west of Hayti, and of course far out of the way of Samana, which is six degrees east of New York. The trade of Vera Cruz and the Gulf States passes between the Florida Keys and Cuba—being much the shortest distance—and, when returning north, of course all vessels seek to secure the considerable advantage of the Gulf stream. The perils of foreign ownership of the West India islands have not hitherto crippled American shipping, and are not likely to embarrass it in the least hereafter. No trade passing to Louisiana, Texas, or Mexico would for a moment call at the bay of Samana, lying easterly and far out of the way, while the "Windward passage" also lies west even of Hayti and east of the most easterly part of Cuba. Only the "Mona passage" lies east of Santo Domingo, and the commerce taking this route is mainly that small amount which goes in the direction of Venezuela.

The fact that the Tennessee, sent out on a national mission, with five hundred men and nine alert newspaper reporters on board, was as much lost to the world for the long period of thirty-three days as though she had been navigating in the open Polar sea, exhibits in the strongest light the absence of trade and ships in the route to Samana, and also its useless remoteness as a harbor for us or any other nation. The bay, too shallow for ships even of the second class, like the Tennessee, to approach within three miles of the shores to receive coal, and proverbially unhealthy, offers no protection whatever to American shipping interests. Whenever those interests may need protection, it will be only in time of war, and none but active cruisers, ships of war not afraid to venture forth out of harbors, would there be of any service. A navy cooped up in the bay of Samana and defended by powerful shore batteries, might be out of the reach of an enemy, but it would be of no value to any exposed commerce. Vessels of war go forth to fight, not to seek shelter.

If we need a naval station in the West Indies, do we not need one much more in the Mediterranean? Really we need nothing of the sort anywhere. The Algerine and other pirates on the coast of Africa have seen something of the American Navy, and will not be likely to forget it. Commerce is as safe there as in Chesapeake bay. In the China seas or Japan there is far more reason for a naval station than here at home, where we have on our own shores any number of good and safe harbors, and which are more formidable to a foreign enemy than Samana could be made by an expenditure of millions. The acquisition of Samana bay was originally based upon a supposed necessity discovered by Secretary Seward, and which really temporarily existed during a time when all of our southern harbors were held by rebels; but no sane man can suppose such a condition of affairs is to be again apprehended and provided for, and if it were to be apprehended, future traitors might be expected to obtain quicker and easier possession of Samana—like another Norfolk—than of Mobile, Pensacola, Savannah, or Charleston. Samana may be safely dismissed with the rebellion, and with it the countless millions of expenditure which a great oceanic naval station would involve.

But it is insisted that we want a naval station in the bay of Samana for the security of our commerce. The baselessness of this assumption will be further seen from the fact that we have, and can have, but the merest pittance of commerce which can ever display itself in that harbor. It all goes and must go further west or further east. To reach Samana, even the trade which now goes nearest must sail two hundred and forty miles out of the way to reach this out of the way station, and then sail back again two hundred and forty miles—making in all a voyage of four hundred and eighty miles—to no purpose; for when Samana is thus reached the only business is, and would be, to get away, as the bay is as empty as that part of the Lake Gennesaret, where Simon Peter and his partners, James and John, toiled all night taking nothing. Besides, if a harbor were needed, unless we were at war with Hayti, there are other harbors far more convenient near at hand—Gonaives, St. Marc, Port au Prince, and, if not at war with Great Britain, there is a fine harbor directly in the route of commerce, at Kingston, Jamaica. It is not likely we shall be at war with either of the countries named, certainly not with both, unless we should ourselves inspire the cause by an act of petty larceny, and be caught with Santo Domingo in our pockets. If we merely want harbors for peaceful commerce they are to be had for nothing, ever gratuitously open to our use.

Before we can possibly need a naval station at Samana we must build up commerce there, and then create a naval fleet to be placed there for its protection; a course not unlike that of the boy who buys a dear purse before he has anything to put in it. We have no commerce now in Santo Domingo; but it is assumed that if we only provide for its protection, though it would need no such protection if we had it, that it would spring forth as miraculously as the gushing water from the rock touched by the rod of Moses. Our greatest foreign commerce is with Liverpool, and yet that port is three thousand miles away from any naval station of the United States. It is quite apparent, if we are strong at home, that our flag alone will protect us anywhere abroad. Respect is inspired by the banner which represents power in reserve, rather than by a few guns floating in distant seas, and which could not float whenever a larger number of hostile guns appeared. National plunderers, as well as private corsairs of the ocean, have disappeared before the march of modern civilization, and treaties of amity and commerce now guard the trade of the world.

Can it be pretended that we need Samana for the purpose of national defense, when we have nothing there, unless we first place it there, to defend? Who is to attack us? Who threatens in the background? Nobody! If Great Britain may rely upon the security that the "streak of silver sea" affords, we know that for the United States the broad Atlantic is a much more impassable bulwark. But in order to make Samana a defensive point we have first to go two thousand miles to fortify it, and then go there to be defended. We leave places of safety to find shelter where weaker nations are our equals, where many naval Powers are our superiors, and where the climate gives the black man very little quarter, and the white man none at all.

The plea that we want the harbor of Samana for any purpose is only a link in the evidence that Hayti, not Santo Domingo, is really coveted and sought, for the harbors of Hayti only could furnish any real accommodation, being far better and less remote. The air in the bay is stagnant, and not even freshened by the trade winds, as the bay is so land-locked that they do not penetrate beyond its mouth. On shore the land front has been gobbled up by the perpetual leases obtained by such diligent seekers of thrift as Fabens, O'Sullivan, and Cazneau.

We are asked to buy the site, next to improve and fortify it, and then to occupy it with a naval fleet, with the vain idea that we might thus fire the languid brains and torpid muscles of the Dominicans to make sugar, grow coffee, and hack down the mahogany trees in such incredible quantities as to glut the world with their exports. We are asked to launch one expenditure which drags after it numerous others of greater and constantly increasing magnitude, and all for the desperate purpose of establishing a permanent commerce and American institutions where nothing has been permanent but failures and revolutions, or for the even more desperate purpose of finding security for our Republic by making fast to a tropical island, whose foundations have been often shaken by earthquakes, and which is scarred all over with the political as well as atmospherical hurricanes of previous centuries.

The frank-spoken sailor, Commander Selfridge, in one of his letters to the Secretary of the Navy, July 14, 1869, starts most unpleasant suggestions. He writes:

"If it is the desire of the Government to possess a port in the island of Hayti either by purchase or lease, I know of no port in the West Indies in convenience of approach, facility of defense, salubrity of position, or of strategic situation, that the port of Nicola Mole, on the northwestern extremity of Hayti, possesses. Now is the most propitious time for negotiation.

"Salnave must have money, and a gift of a worn-out monitor or two would hasten matters.

"While my short stay in the island will not permit me to speak with authority, it is my individual opinion that if the United States should annex Hayti on the representation of a party it would be found an elephant both costly in money and lives."

I have no doubt that nine tenths of our officers, both military and naval, if called upon, would testify that, even with an expenditure of millions, the bay of Samana would be a source of weakness to the United States.

It should also be noted when we have got our naval vessels into the torrid zone—and all of Santo Domingo is within that zone—that by the regulations of the Navy our men cease from labor and are permitted to hire natives to attend to the ship, a privilege not likely to remain a dead letter among "old salts." Let me quote from the regulations of the United States Navy for 1870 to officers commanding vessels:

"222. In cruising in the torrid zone he may engage the natives to attend the ship and carry provisions and water, if it should be advisable to do so in order to preserve the health of the crew."

Would it not be more advisable to preserve the health of the crew, and our own moral and political health as well, by letting Santo Domingo severely alone? If the Navy must be permitted to employ natives to do even ordinary work on shipboard, who will our agriculturists, miners, and mechanics, who may be seduced to go there, find it advisable to employ to do the extraordinary work of supporting "ten millions of people in luxury," which the President has intimated can be done?

LAND ENOUGH ALREADY.

Although I have never had any filibustering ideas as to the manifest destiny or miraculous growth of our country, I yet have an abiding faith in the prospective character and greatness of the people of America, however territorially bounded. It is true that territorial expansions have some undefinable fascinations for the Anglo-Saxon race, and they are not to be wholly proscribed as wicked, for they are sometimes innocent; but the merest tyro cannot blink out of sight the fact that gross bulk, or geographical extent, is not the only nor the most vital element which figures in the estimate of a great and enlightened nation. The intelligence and the virtue, the industry and the courage, the intellect and the stamina of the people, not the sum total of their property in dirt, form the grander part of the basis upon which rest the claims of all nations to rank among their contemporaries or in the history that survives their end.

If the question now were barely the acquisition of more land, unincumbered by population—although we have land enough and to spare, homesteads even to give away—it would have an aspect somewhat less objectionable.

Then it would be merely the cost of protection to the additional territory, the transfer of some portion of our own people to the new locality, and the risk of their too probable speedy deterioration of character. But when embarrassed with a population, having, too, a most unattractive history and character, we have a more serious and complex proposition to consider and determine. Will the population elevate or depress the standard of American civilization? Will it prove such an enterprise as to attract the good or the bad? Will it tend to secure or imperil the life of our republican institutions? I would not speak disrespectfully of the Dominicans, if there was anything of which I could speak respectfully. I would not speak of them at all if it were not proposed to take them into our Union as equal copartners.

THE POOR CHARACTER OF DOMINICANS.

But the people of Dominica are confessedly in the lowest state of poverty, and must remain so forever, because they will not work. They are grossly ignorant; and must remain so, because they have no aspiration to be otherwise, have attended no schools themselves, nor will they provide any for their children. They are a foreign, incompatible race, and never can become homogeneous, in manners or customs, language or religion, with our people; because, having a diverse and incoherent origin, and a climate always tending to effeminacy, they have also for ages been intermixed with a stock which neither learns virtues nor forgets vices, and which clings with the sublimest faith to revolutions and the Catholic priesthood of Santo Domingo. There can be no attraction here for any other class of emigrants than those to be found in a similar latitude, where numbers may have diminished the spontaneous supplies of food, or a class unwilling to starve and yet not quite willing to work.

The Dominican people have been represented to be of such inferior and flexible material that they could be at once molded and governed by a thousand, or even fifty, Americans. If that were so, what fifty, of what city, would be likely to land there first? Would they pour forth from the fertile loins of Mackerelville or Northern Liberties? Would they be of a character fit to be intrusted with equal powers as a State in peace or war to checkmate Massachusetts or New York or Ohio? Surely such a consummation no more commends itself to the older States than to the younger, and could give us neither strength nor renown at home nor abroad. Let us thank God that our patriotism does not yet teach us to love Dominica as we love New York, Massachusetts, or Ohio.

The Santo Domingo chiefs, judging them by their public acts, seem to be not greatly in advance of their subjects, and are ready to sell their country when in power, or to fight for it when out of power. Their love of despotic rule and lust for gold equals that of the most graceless tyrants of any race, but they seem to be utterly destitute of that noble ambition which seeks to elevate their people, or which enthrones liberty, justice, and law as the highest aim of human government.

A people wholly without education, led in factions by unprincipled and desperate chiefs, destitute of all ambition which a high civilization inspires, reeking in filth and laziness, regardless of marriage or its binding power, who never invented anything nor comprehended the use of the inventions of others, whose virtue is indexed by a priesthood elevated by no scrap of learning and wretchedly debauched in morals, would prove a serious political and moral as well as financial incumbrance. It cannot be reckoned statesmanship to add to the complications of the hour by going abroad after fresh elements of inevitable vexation and discord. By any treaty Santo Domingo must be permitted to come into our system *on an equal footing with other Territories to be admitted in due time as a State;* or if admitted by joint resolution it must take position at once as a State. It must have Representatives and Senators in due time, or at once.

We cannot have even the poor privilege of starting a plan of government with a military satrap at its head, clothed with such prerogatives as might be necessary to control a people, if not barbaric, at least unaccustomed to a free Government or a free religion, and wholly illiterate and superstitious. Whether we were to permit such a population, wholly incapable of governing themselves, to a share in governing us, and we have no constitutional precedents for anything else, nor will anything else be authorized, or whether we alone were to govern them, it would be found equally objectionable and inharmonious. We cannot afford to dilute the aggregate intelligence of our own people below its present standard while we are striving to elevate that standard; nor ought we to embark in a wild scheme of planting colonial governors around the world, in an age when they have almost ceased to be tolerated. Let us educate and train the four million pupils which Providence has recently placed in our charge before we take up a much more hopeless class, that is to say, the ragged school of Dominica. Honor most clearly does not lie in pushing American institutions in the direction of the equator, where even freedom's purest metal yields to the fervent heat. Even the American Republic cannot "lie immortal in the arms of fire."

NO ANNEXATION TOLERABLE EXCEPT NORTHWARD.

But let us for a moment turn our eyes from a land congenial to monkeys and parrots to something of more substantial value. Let us forego the seductions of sugar and coffee plantations, rising so luxuriantly in some tropical imaginations, though scarcely to be found now even in the narrow *cul-de-sac* they once filled, and face the north.

"The blood more stirs
"To rouse a lion than to start a hare."

At the north there is a country interlocked and dovetailed to our northern boundary, throughout its whole magnificent extent, with a people of kindred stock and tongue, which, without money and without price, and with their own consent, will at some time surely show, perhaps in the second term of General Grant, that they are ready to join and improve their fortunes by going hand in hand and abreast with the Great Republic. Let them do this, and their advancement will be assured, while our own will not be retarded, but perhaps made more complete. This would reflect honor upon all parties, banish Fenianism, and blot out the name of the Alabama.

The British provinces are of age, and Great Britain daily hints to the bashful youngsters that, although she will not forbid them all shelter under the paternal roof and will not wholly cease the great baby perquisites of soft caresses, yet she feels chagrined that they have not discovered it to be quite time for them to shift for themselves and to cease teasing her for bonbons and pocket-money. She does not tell them in plain words, as Isaac told Jacob, where and when to go and wed, for she is altogether too clever not to know what alliance has been foreordained and determined. What the laws of the universe join together cannot be kept asunder. It will not be a runaway match, for there is no shame and need be no secrecy about it; but some fine morning, the last of the "Queen's Own" having departed, the New Dominion will muster its manhood and pop the question. After that, at Toronto, Montreal, Halifax, and Quebec, we shall hear from more than four million throats, "Hail Columbia!" Here is the true field of honor. But, if we show an indiscriminate and promiscuous desire to annex anything and everything, even a slice of a tropical island, a match of the cheapest and most dubious character, how can we expect our proud and fastidious Anglo-Saxon neighbors on the north, ripe in experience and liberal culture, with their solid and extensive patrimony, to join such a union with any alacrity or affection?

I am sincerely apprehensive that the project for Dominican annexation will seriously jeopardize our prospects in the North, and perhaps postpone the interests and happiness of millions of people indefinitely. The northern field of enterprise, which might attract our people and capital, would be one of assured health and profit, and contribute to the power, certainly not to the weakness, of the nation. The New Dominion, once infolded by our flag, would find the blood coursing in its veins with a swifter current and fuller pulsation, and with all her industries, her commerce, and national improvements, upheld by forty million hearty coadjutors, would also find such security and prosperity as have not been reached even in the dreams of its most sanguine citizens. Its population and wealth would be doubled in a single decade. Why should we, then, barricade the entrance to our Union against the provinces on the north by any rubbish tumbled in from the West India Islands? We urge nothing—are in no hurry—but let us not snatch at half an island and lose a continent.

THE SEWARD BATCH OF TREATIES ALL BAD.

The present Administration was so unfortunate as to receive as a legacy from the late versatile Secretary of State, Mr. Seward, a series of great treaties for petty annexation and petty reciprocity, which contributed, perhaps, more to the self-satisfaction of the Secretary than they appear destined to contribute to that of the country he officially represented. Not one of these infelicitous treaties had its origin with the present Administration, which owes to them no original fealty whatsoever. That with Denmark, for the annexation of St. Thomas—in close proximity with Santo Domingo—seems to have been vulnerable to the first ocean earthquake, and has been, perhaps not inopportunely, swallowed up by a series of those great disturbers of "the best laid plans" of diplomacy, while little Denmark, unwittingly trusting to an unadvised treaty and the fair words of our Secretary, suffers the shame of those who stumble and then hastily look around to see if the world's fingers are not pointed at them. Our national position has been awkward and ungracious; but what could we do? One thing was clear; we did not want St. Thomas, unless we were to take it, as we might Santo Domingo, and throw it back again into the sea.

The inception of these treaties under President Johnson was widely at variance with the course pursued by Jefferson in 1803 in the case of Louisiana, and of Monroe in 1819 in the case of Florida. They started with legislative concurrence. They got the consent of Congress beforehand, and, to quote the language of the late Senator Benton, "the treaty-making power was but the instrument of the legislative will." Besides, the subject then in hand underwent public discussion. There were no secrets. The people understood what they wanted and what was on foot.

Manifestly, in so important a step this was and is now the proper course. If the treaty-making power, working in secret and wholly irresponsible, may totally disregard the public judgment, then republican or popular government is a farce.

THE "MONROE DOCTRINE" INTERPRETED.

There has been so much loose talk on the subject of the "Monroe doctrine," so called, that President Grant may have been justified—I think he was—in making an earnest experiment to find out its practical meaning or how it is to be understood by the present generation. It has by some been held to include much more than I think the simple declaration warranted. As read by me it only declared "America no longer open to European colonization;" not that we wanted to colonize. President Monroe only desired that all parts of America might have a chance to be independent and republican if they chose, without any European hinderance or interference, and those refractory Spanish-American colonies, which Spain was then striving to coerce, were objects that challenged our own as well as a world-wide solicitude. The doctrine was not that we were to seize all the land adjoining us, nor was it by any means susceptible of the selfish interpretation that European vultures were to be driven away in order that the American eagle might swoop down and clutch the prey.

The wise founders of our Republic contemplated a simple form of government, one imposing the smallest possible burdens, upon which it would be wholly incompatible to ingraft a system of colonies or outlying dependencies. A large navy, without which the defense of colonies or distant States would be impossible, was regarded by our fathers with great distrust. Jefferson, in his simplicity, only wanted gun-boats; but Jefferson never sought to colonize or to annex distant islands. He sought to make bone of our bone and flesh of our flesh the great delta of the Mississippi. It remained for our late Secretary of State, always grand in his conceptions, even when wrong, first to grasp the north pole, and then to leap back almost to the equator, or to alternate between icebergs and earthquakes. In his world-traveling eye not only "the whole boundless continent" was ours, but all of its outlying incoherent dependencies were equally to be coveted. Strange that any Republican administration should have been lured by such doubtful baits!

But Jefferson only coveted Louisiana, holding the great outlet of the Mississippi and our most magnificent domains lying west of that river, which it was desirable to have at any cost, even at the price, he said, of an amendment to the Constitution, if necessary.

In the case of Florida, it was the home of the Seminoles, whose predatory warfare could not be repelled without following them within the boundaries of a foreign Government, involving a double war, and, therefore, this territory, contiguous to our southern boundary, had to be acquired as a measure of prospective peace rather than of aggrandizement, though it resulted in a most expensive Indian war.

Texas was largely settled by our own people, and the geographical homogeniety between that country and the United States made it a tempting acquisition. The people of Texas were unanimously in favor of annexation, and being an *independent State* it was claimed, with more adroitness than integrity, that Congress had the constitutional right to admit such *States* into the Union. Annexation was an issue made at the presidential election, and the candidate in favor of annexation had succeeded, whether that was the decisive issue or not. The people of the North and West, it is true, opposed it because the message of President Tyler in December, 1843, "squinted at war with both" Great Britain and Mexico, in order to obtain it. Beyond that our people were vehemently opposed to it on the ground that it was a sinister and premeditated extension of the area of slavery. They were opposed to it on account of the sham proposal to "reannex" territory which never belonged to us. They were opposed to it because "an army of observation," not a fleet in the bay of Samana, was sent into it, and then a false declaration made that "war existed by the act of Mexico." They were opposed to it because of the threat of South Carolina that, if not annexed to the *United* States, it should be annexed to the *slave-holding* States.

Our treaty with Great Britain, commonly known as the Clayton and Bulwer treaty, made April 19, 1850, fully illustrates the American construction of the Monroe doctrine, so called, when it was restrained by the limits of sanity and sound statesmanship. Although the particular object of this treaty was to secure a ship-canal from the Atlantic to the Pacific ocean, yet it declares that the high contracting parties "not only desired, in entering into this convention, to accomplish a particular object, but also to establish a general principle," and if they had not in words so declared the compact then made established a precedent upon which a general principle finds an impregnable basis. It was provided that neither Great Britain nor the United States will ever occupy or fortify or colonize, or assume or exercise any dominion over Nicaragua, Costa Rica, the Mosquito coast, or any part of Central America. This is a most important and emphatic enunciation of the general policy of the United States, and evinced our willingness to be excluded from all dominion over territory in the direction of the tropics, outside of our present limits, provided European nations were also to be excluded. It is a positive renunciation of the wild policy of territorial expansion in the direction named. Here a bit was put in the mouth of our own prancing nag of "manifest destiny," and Great Britain was forced to abandon her legacy from the pretended Mosquito king, of laced-coat and cocked-hat memory; and that was all and just what we most desired. Who ever heard that treaty denounced as any violation of the Monroe doctrine? Nobody!

HAYTI WANTS SANTO DOMINGO; WE DON'T.

Santo Domingo is a portion of an island

greatly coveted by Hayti, from which it was violently wrenched in 1844, and to which it geographically belongs, as truly as Louisiana, Florida, and Texas belonged to the United States. Hayti wants it, claims never to have abandoned it, and in due time might probably have it, unless prevented by extraneous interference. Our good will might be profitably extended to both; we might fairly encourage legitimate commerce, of which we should get little, but not an illegitimate, entangling, and indissoluble alliance, of which we should get too much. The addition to us would be poor indeed; but, added to Hayti, it might tend to build up a home and a Government of greater promise to the liberty and welfare of a large portion of the colored race in the West India islands. To aid such an enterprise would be a mission worthy of our high position. The colored race are entitled to try the experiment of practical independence. Their civilization should not be cramped and overshadowed by holding them forever in contact with a superior race. For us to rob them of their only opportunity in the West India islands puts the risk of their final shipwreck upon us, and gives to them no scope for the exercise of self-reliance or for the development of their natural growth.

We stand in no need of it because of any surplus population from which it is desirable to be disincumbered. If there is any purpose to have the colored race expatriated from the continent at least it is not now avowed. Emigration to the new States now draws heavily upon the older States. These new States and Territories, upon which we expend and must expend millions for their development and protection, and the southern States, which have recently had a new birth, have a right to every surplus man, and every surplus dollar which can be spared from all the other States. They should not be made to stand back for an unnatural flirtation in the tropics, discreditable to our age and dignity. Our affection, as well as our interest, should constrain us to husband all our resources, not at present any too abundant, for the improvement of our broadly extended but unsettled estates. Do we want sugar and cotton lands? Have we not got them in abundance in Texas, in Arkansas, in South Carolina, in Mississippi, in Louisiana, in Alabama, and in Florida? Who wants to build up a foreign insular El Dorado to compete with these States, and proclaim, as we must if we are in earnest, that they are worthless in comparison with Santo Domingo? Is it to be preferred that the tide of people from the North and East, now setting so strongly toward the West, and which would tend southward also if the States there would respond to the President's hearty desire and "let us have peace," is it to be preferred, I say, that this tide should be diverted by the fiction of crops without labor, spontaneous sugar, coffee, and tobacco—forgetful that light labor in the torrid zone is more exhausting than heavy labor in the temperate zone, and that any crops must be intermingled with black vomit and yellow fever, with poisonous insects, and other pests too numerous to mention, all equally the spontaneous fruits of Santo Domingo? Justice to ourselves requires that we should take care of what we have at home before we scatter abroad.

OUR FUTURE GROWTH.

Some speculative political economists indulge in predictions about the future vastness of our population; but is it not preposterous to expect our past ratio of increase for an indefinite length of time? When the best lands shall be exhausted, as we may find at some time they will be, and certainly when our population becomes dense, it would be unphilosophical and contrary to all history to expect the same ratio of increase from births, nor could we hope the same increase from immigration.

There will be a declension in the power to absorb as well as in the sources of supply. During the fiscal year 1870 we received 387,098 immigrants. Since 1847, only twenty three years, the number of foreigners who have made our country their home amounts to 4,297,980. Our present population, but for such accessions, would amount to only one third of what it is now. The difference between receiving and sending out annually 300,000 men is marvelous, and it is a point deserving especial attention. The average cost of raising a man in any civilized country is rather over than under $1,000, and of a woman rather less; but the average is still not less than $1,000. Upon a removal to a new country they augment its capital by the transference of their economical value as future producers and the exchangable value of all property which belongs to them. Our country has been exceptionally enriched by the capital and labor of vast numbers who were reared at the sole expense of others. That greatly enhances the present prosperity of western States, filled with able-bodied men which have not yet been taxed for their infancy or old age. We have thus brought to us annually from abroad a capital of $50,000,000 by persons who add each year by their labor from two to three hundred millions more. To-day portions of Germany sorely feel a comparative loss, and are studying—certainly Austrian statesmen have been studying—how to prevent this annoying depletion which may so disastrously affect their wealth and power as a people.

Santo Domingo could not be of the slightest value to us unless repeopled and supplied with capital, to be subtracted from our home stock or accepted as questionable foreign gifts—the spawn of the Caribbean sea and the Mexican Gulf. Any gain there would be either so much positive loss at home or a gain of numbers with a loss of character. Although the task is as hopeless as would be the resuscitation of Tyre or Sidon, Carthage or Babylon, if it were possible, could we afford it? Shall we postpone the great destinies of Kansas, Iowa, and Nebraska, of Colorado and Montana, and the youthful and vigorous States on the Pacific coast, until we can plant and hatch out a new brood of States in distant seas? New Orleans and Baltimore, Philadelphia and New York, Boston and San Francisco, are very considerable sea-ports. Can we expect to rival them in Santo Domingo? Does any one suppose that our people would add anything to their own wealth or length of days by going there, rather than by accepting the opportunities to be found in our own rich and many-sided domains? Here experience is our guide, and we do not risk all on an experiment, already, time and again, exploded. Here we stand on *terra firma*, with no ghost of failure rising up to confront our faith and progress. Let us remember, even if we forget many earlier destructive visitations, that so late as 1842 the shores of Santo Domingo to the extent of sixty miles were submerged in consequence of earthquakes. In 1770 an earthquake in Hayti destroyed Port au Prince. What has been may be again. But these shocks, however much to be dreaded, are not more portentous than the shock to be apprehended to our political system from a misalliance with one or all of the West India islands. The annexations, safely tolerated in the youth of the Republic, may not be so freely indulged as we reach maturity, when the accumulated debt of all the toil and excesses of both youth and age, past and present, must be met and paid at the same moment.

STATISTICS EXCELLENT IF TRUE.

We have been cited in most respectable quarters to some chronicles as to the ancient magnitude of the trade of Santo Domingo, and I may be pardoned for saying that we might just as well be cited to those concerning ancient Venice or Carthage. When commerce has once forsaken any place, does history show that, under any circumstances, it has ever returned? But are there not good reasons for suspecting the solidity as well as the veracity of any history which puts forth a claim to one hundred millions of exports at any time past, present, or to come, for Santo Domingo? By exposure to a little criticism such figures will shrink up amazingly, and what in magnitude appeared to be a camel may turn out after all only a very small weasel.

Let it be admitted that at one period of time, and about 1789, the trade of Santo Domingo was quite large, but of course it included that of Hayti, for Santo Domingo only dates its independence from 1844, which is yet unacknowledged by Hayti. The articles produced there were luxuries, to some extent of only recent extensive use, and being in great demand bore enormous prices. To make up the gross amount of their exports it will be seen, from the table I give, that cotton is reckoned at thirty-four cents per pound, muscovado sugar at seventy-four cents per pound, and coffee at eighteen and a half cents per pound. The number of ships engaged, it is also true, was large, (sixteen hundred it has even been claimed,) but their size must have been very small. Their great port, the city of Santo Domingo, admits nothing else, or ships only of the fourth class or less. One steamship of the present day would be equal to a score and more of the vessels then ordinarily employed. The island was then the great distributing point for French commerce and exchange, or the commercial metropolis of the New World, just as St. Thomas has recently been the seat of a considerable trade from being practically a free port, although itself actually producing nothing; a trade that would be annihilated by the imposition of even the most trivial taxation.

Statistics are excellent if they are truthful, but when embellished with fictions or distorted by the wrinkles of age they are merely mathematical monstrosities. I might quote Malte Brun, James Redpath, who resided there for some time, and many other authorities, but McCulloch's Geographical Dictionary is accounted rather higher statistical authority than the work, so often quoted and relied upon in this case, of the malignant Tory author of Alison's History, which, it will be remembered, so elaborately libels America and the Americans. The historian who identifies republicanism with the powers of hell may have been a prodigy in conic sections and fluxions, but he is not therefore to be always trusted in the simpler forms of facts and figures. "What is history," said Napoleon, "but a fiction agreed upon?" But this of Sir Archibald's, relied upon by the Senator from Indiana and also by the Senator from Michigan, I may say, is not agreed upon. I will therefore give McCulloch's table of "exports of the French part of Santo Domingo during each of three years ending in 1789," including the very year when the exports were largest, and when they have been, as Senators will remember, claimed to be a hundred millions, or a greater amount than we find to have been exported by nearly all of North America thirty or forty years afterward:

		Livres.
Clayed sugar, pounds	58,642,214	41,049,549
Muscovado sugar, pounds	8,659,829	34,619,931
Coffee, pounds	71,663,187	71,663,187
Cotton, pounds	6,698,858	12,397,716
Indigo, pounds	951,607	8,534,463
Molasses, hogsheads	23,061	2,767,320
Rum, hogsheads	2,600	312,000
Raw hides, number	6,500	52,000
Tanned hides, number	7,900	118,500
Total value in livres		171,544,666
Total value in sterling		£1,765,129
Or, in United States money		$8,825,625

This, it should be noted, was in the years of the very highest prosperity—embracing the western end and the only end of the island that ever had any prosperity—and is really but a trifle more than the small city of Portland, Maine, sends annually over the Grand Trunk railroad. Yet it is the prop for sixteen hundred vessels and a hundred millions of exports in the past and in expectancy!

DOMINICAN EXPORT BUBBLES.

Let me call attention to the fact that the greatest number of people in Santo Domingo at the time of the greatest amount of commerce was 400,000 slaves, 25,000 whites, and 25,000 mulattoes, and then bear in mind the fact that the United States in 1830 contained a population of 12,866,020. No one will deny our own activity, whether as to production or trade, and yet our whole exports then amounted only to $73,819,508, or less by more than twenty-six million dollars than 425,000 working tatterdemalions in Santo Domingo are represented to have exported in 1789! With a population of 17,069,453 in 1840, our exports amounted to only $104,805,891, and yet it is assumed that in proportion to numbers the Dominicans in 1789 exceeded the United States in its products exported in the ratio of *thirty eight* to *one*. Need I say more touching the Dominican bubble, or the hundred millions of exports which would gush forth by only hoisting the American flag?

Even by the coercion of the military police of Toussaint L'Ouverture, when every man not a proprietor was compelled to hire himself as a laborer to some agricultural proprietor, and to work from sunrise to sunset, they were only able to raise the value of the products to one third of the amount of 1789, and when the restraint was removed in 1825, under Boyer, the exports for the entire island dropped to the pitiful sum of four shillings two pence for each inhabitant.

It may be a proper question to ask, what does the trade of this part of the island now amount to? Is it not curious that even British statisticians, proverbially painstaking, make no separate account of it, but include it with that of Hayti, of the two by far the most considerable? Like gold dust it has first to be caught up with something else, or by quicksilver, before you can find or estimate it at all. The latest returns I have found of the trade of Hayti and Santo Domingo combined, in British documents, are as follows:

	Total imports.	*Exports.*
1861	£137,471	£310,555
1862	151,719	474,842
1863	276,610	545,142
1864	251,210	459,876
1865	230,287	348,419

Instead of one hundred millions from Santo Domingo, the exports, including those of Hayti, amount to no more than from one and a half to two million and a half of dollars, and of this it would be more than liberal to allow that even one quarter belongs to Santo Domingo. In 1868 the imports of Santo Domingo from the United States, according to our own records, were $83,363, and the exports to the United States $64,110. Yet, with these beggarly but indisputable facts before us, it is seriously argued that a few dashing Americans would work out the miracle of giving us a trade only surpassed at present in its vast magnitude by that of the United States with Great Britain! I may say with the Prince of Denmark—

"They fool me to the top of my bent."

It appears also that a firm in New York, Spofford Brothers, now own and run a line of steamers under a grant to a Mr. Funkhouser, with a provision that five per cent. of the import and export dues on all merchandise carried by said line between New York and New Orleans and the Dominican republic be allowed to the owners of the steamers. Pray, how would such a grant be disposed of by us?

The Senator from Indiana, in a former debate, took pains to quote from an official document the amount of our trade with Cuba and Porto Rico, and to contrast it with that of the British American possessions and Mexico. It is large, it is true, and somewhat larger than the latter altogether. The figures of the first, including exports and imports, were $88,102,670, and of the last only $72,000,000. But for what purpose does the Senator array these figures? Santo Domingo will not blot out or supply the place of Cuba and Porto Rico, and if such a result were possible it could give us no larger market for our products. The torrid zone everywhere furnishes only limited markets. They consume little, and that little, it happens, can be mainly obtained elsewhere at less cost than from us. If the contrast was intended to be unfavorable to the trade of the British possessions and Mexico, then it was a mistake, for the reason that while our exports to Cuba and Porto Rico are small, they are in proportion to imports much larger to the Dominion and other North American British possessions. So far as they concern the Santo Domingo question, the figures so prominently put forth are without any logical significance. I fancy they were intended to give the impression that the balance of trade would be made all right through the annexation of Santo Domingo, and in that view they are *entitled*—I say it with all respect—to about as much consideration as we should give to the toy blocks of children, with which they sometimes build barns, forts, or churches, as it may best please juvenile architects. The Dominican block-house is of about equal substance and of equal ingenuity.

Usually the Register of the United States appears to follow the British example in making up the report of the trade of Hayti and San Domingo, and combines them together, not considering the latter worthy of any separate notice; but in 1868 a separate account was kept, and we find our domestic exports to Hayti were $2.956,983, and of foreign goods reëxported $299,619, while our domestic exports to Santo Domingo were only $64,110, and but $2,091 of foreign goods reëxported. Our imports for the same year from Hayti were $760,087, and from Santo Domingo only $83,363; the trade with Santo Domingo thus leaving a balance of about twenty thousand dollars to be paid by us in gold, while the Haytien trade was exceedingly healthful, leaving a balance of $2,196,896 to be paid to us in gold. A critical examination of the trade of Santo Domingo has been provoked, and its absolute nullity, therefore, deserves to be fully exposed. Its consequence has been magnified by being confounded with that of Hayti, although the trade of that little republic is quite restricted. Of coffee we imported in 1868 from Hayti 4,631181 pounds, and from Santo Domingo only 21.815 pounds. From Hayti we imported 30,827 pounds cocoa and 219,098 pounds of cotton, but none from Santo Domingo. Of sugar we got $20,092 worth from Hayti, and $10,111 worth from Santo Domingo. Of dye-woods we received from Hayti to the amount of $419,442, and how much do you think, Mr. President, from Santo Domingo? Remember the immense forests we have been told about, only requiring a few blows of the woodman's ax to ship countless cargoes! The amount, all told, was to the value of $15,988!

Nearly half of all our imports from Santo Domingo were in two items—$16,326 in mahogany, and $22,029 in lignum-vitæ. Why, sir, some of the farmers not many miles from this capital do nearly as large a business every winter in cutting and selling cord-wood! It would be eclipsed by the trade of mere boys in Michigan or Maine! Of tropical fruits—and here certainly we ought to find a surfeit, their growth is so luxuriant, so entirely laborless!—the amount we have to acknowledge is twenty-one dollars for ripe fruits and eight dollars for preserved fruits! The owner of a California garden would feel himself treated unhandsomely if a single visitor should not consume or carry away more than our whole year's importation from Santo Domingo! Here are the facts taken from our own documents. Mr. President, contrast them with the hundred million theory—"the house that Jack built"—which grave Senators have indorsed in this Chamber! Do they warrant such extravagant predictions?

COCOANUTS AND BANANAS WILL NOT PAY OFF THE PUBLIC DEBT.

If we may accept the theory of the President in his annual message, the annexation of Santo Domingo would be the appropriate plaster, not only for nearly all our national sores, but for those of other lands. It would be a cure for many evils at home—naval, military, financial, moral, commercial, and political—as well as the precursor of reforms greatly needed abroad. A panacea of such extensive pretensions is commonly found upon trial of small virtue anywhere, and certainly cannot be counted upon where it has signally failed when tested by other parties, as Santo Domingo often has been by other nations.

The opinions of the President of the United States, official and personal, are entitled to great consideration; and having given them that consideration, both from duty and inclination, I feel that they must be adopted or rejected, with perfect independence, as God enables us to see the right. The message asserts of this measure that—

"It is to provide honest means of paying our honest debts without overtaxing the people."

But how? The President is too much in earnest to deal in jokes, and this must be treated as a serious matter. It seems to be argued that annexation would enable the United States to obtain from Santo Domingo all of our sugar, coffee, tobacco, and tropical fruits; and it is then stated that—

"The production of our own supply of these articles will cut off more than one hundred millions of our annual imports, besides largely increasing our exports. With such a picture it is easy to see how our large debt abroad is ultimately to be extinguished."

The colors of this picture are positive and very brilliant, but can they be warranted not to fade when exposed to the sunlight of facts and figures? How would it do for a Secretary of the Treasury to entertain such speculative visions? Treasury estimates must be built upon the solid data of ascertained facts. The imagination is a poor financier, wholly without thrift and great only in gigantic disbursements. Let alone the grand assumption as to the capacity of Santo Domingo to produce all the articles enumerated—eclipsing Cuba, Porto Rico, and all the sugar countries of the world—not stopping even to deny the averment of the message that it is "capable of supporting ten millions of people in luxury," how are these vast products when grown to be covered into the Treasury of the United States?

Supposing the fertility of the soil and the disposition to labor not to be overstated, when annexation shall come to pass, the sugar, coffee, tobacco, and tropical fruits produced there, much or little, would nevertheless be the property of private owners, and must be paid for accordingly, and the price would be the average price of such articles in the chief marts of the world, but not less than the cost of production in Santo Domingo. If the world's supply of coffee and sugar were to be so largely increased, however, by a hundred millions, then it is plain to see that the price might be greatly diminished; so much so, perhaps, as to make the cultivation of such crops, even in Santo Domingo, unprofitable, and then their curtailment or total abandonment must speedily follow. Sugar has been a profitable crop in Cuba when cultivated by over six hundred and fifty thousand slaves, the slave trade replacing the enormous losses caused by the annual mortality of the laborers; but it has not been profitable in Hayti since Haytien independence, nor in the British West Indies since emancipation. Is it to be expected that Americans in such a climate can successfully compete with the cheap labor of Cuba, Brazil, or India?

Still keeping the "picture" before us, that all of our sugar, tobacco, and tropical fruits might be obtained exclusively from the east end of Santo Domingo, it follows then that we must surrender millions of revenue which is now obtained from these sources. How would such a deficit be made up? Manifestly it could only be done by levying an equal amount upon tea, salt, or some other articles imported from foreign countries. A certain amount of revenue is indispensable to the existence of the Government. Remove duties from one quarter and they must be put on in some other. If our supply of sugar, coffee, tobacco, and tropical fruits could be obtained free of duties something else must then assume the burden. If our imports of dutiable articles should be diminished one fourth, then a proportionate increase of the tariff upon the remainder must follow or internal taxation must again be resorted to for means to supply the deficiency. No one proposes to resort to the latter at home, and therefore it could not be imposed upon Santo Domingo. With no duties upon our exports to or from Santo Domingo, and no revenue from internal taxation, what becomes of annexation as "an honest means of paying our honest debts?" Beyond all doubt it would cripple our Treasury, and be the signal for the imposition of new taxes at home, and of no insignificant amount, if the dream of cutting off $100,000,000 of imports should ever come to pass. The milk in free cocoanuts will not pay the public debt. I am inflexibly opposed to any increase of taxation and in favor of reducing the present burdens at the earliest day.

The fallacy of expecting any revenue from Santo Domingo may be fitly shown by the example of Cuba with respect to Spain. Spain needs and ever has needed more revenue, and no one will question the zeal with which she has attempted to obtain it. We denounce the Spanish impositions upon Cuba and would not be likly to imitate such rapacity; yet the sum total of that taxation is less than half that borne by the city of New York, and for the latest years I have found prior to their present civil war amounts for *maritime* to $6,721,250, and for *internal* to $5,527,462, or a total of $12,248,712. Nearly all of this is exhausted by the civil, military, naval, and miscellaneous Cuban expenses, Spain only nibbling annually about fifteen hundred thousand dollars, and this sum is really transmitted to Spain in support of legations, pensioners, and employés connected with the island government.

Only *nominally* has she secured this pitiful sum of $1,500,000 of annual revenue, and has actually already sunk a capital in her latest inconclusive effort to suppress the Cuban rebellion, which she cannot hope to recover, or even the interest thereon, from all the future revenues of Cuba, though her sovereignty were to be prolonged for coming ages. Cuba has a population of 1,443,381, of which 662,587 are slaves and 216,176 free colored. Santo Domingo is estimated to contain 120,000 inhabitants, though the late commission estimates it higher, which, if we were to oppress with equal rigor, would yield in proportion, it will be seen, a net revenue of about one hundred and twenty-five thousand dollars. But instead of even this paltry credit we should have millions of expenditures, such as it has cost Spain to establish a doubtful supremacy in Cuba, or Great Britain her less doubtful despotism in Jamaica. Truly, if while our present Administration has been so successfully paying off over $100,000,000 of debt annually, the annexation of Santo Domingo has suddenly become the only mode by which the public debt can be extinguished without overtaxing the people, as the idea would appear to be entertained in most respectable quarters, then our condition is deplorable enough, as that measure, by increasing our expenditures and diminishing our receipts, would really only plunge us into difficulties far deeper and more inextricable than those we are now called upon to confront.

THREATENING INCREASE OF TAXES.

The possession of Santo Domingo would heavily increase national taxes, as it would be absurd to suppose that a country without an acre of public lands, of one hundred and twenty or one hundred and sixty thousand poor Dominican men and women, unaccustomed and unwilling to labor, could or would make even the smallest contribution to the payment of the public debt or even to their own defense. The tracks would all be outgoing from the Treasury, and none incoming. The first thing to be done would be to appoint a Governor, whose staff and surroundings must be equal to those of the captain general of Cuba, and Governor of Jamaica, or he would rank only as one of the "poor white trash," and turn out to be no Governor at all. The judiciary and other branches of the civil service must be furnished, and there would be plenty of room for all the discontented culls thrown out of custom-house employment at home.

Then a permanent naval squadron would be ornamental and contingently indispensable. Docks, arsenals, hospitals, and navy-yards must follow as a matter of course, as Santo Domingo is surrounded by dangerous rivals as well as by dangerous reefs, and our naval squadrons would be in constant dread of barnacles and constant need of repairs. Forts, martello-towers, and other fortifications, would have to bristle up around the whole circuit of the shore lines. How many regiments of soldiers—horse, foot, and dragoons—would find employment and graves there the experience of Governments having similar dependencies sufficiently discloses. Revenue cutters would find an ample field for their prowess, as smugglers would replaçe ancient buccaneers. Rivers and harbors would require improvements; railroads, with subsidies, would turn out to be postal or military necessities. An assay office and mint could hardly be refused to a land of so much undiscovered gold, where they are now compelled to use paper money instead of pieces of leather, such as were in vogue when the mines of Cibao were most productive, and yet yielded but half a million dollars annually to the labor of wretched miners. More than all, schools and school-houses would need to be established with laws making attendance compulsory.

This long catalogue of requirements may seem extensive. But there is not one of them, if a treaty were ratified, that would not at once be loudly called for; and our home people would have to foot the bills. Spain kept an army in Cuba, prior to the late civil war—including infantry, cavalry, and artillery—of twenty-eight thousand men, or nearly as large as that now maintained by the United States, and a navy made up of four frigates, fifteen steam-ships, and thirty-two smaller vessels. This indicates the climate into which it is sought to plunge American institutions!

Such an annexation would expose the peace of the country to new complications and to constant peril. Revolutions and civil discord seem to be the normal condition of the tropics. The doors of the Temple of Janus are never closed near the equator nor in Spanish American republics. The defense in case of war of this patch in the ocean would involve an outlay of men and money greatly in excess of the importance of the territory or of its people; and after all our expenditures, any naval Power, having the most iron-clad vessels at hand, in case of war, would at once become its master; any improvement made by us would only make the prize the more glittering and valuable to the captors.

At home we may be invincible; but as defenders of out-lying dependencies we should drop to a third or fourth-rate Power, because we have not and ought not to have a large navy, for the mere glory of naval supremacy, or the vanity of a comparison with the royal and imperial navies of the Old World. We might, indeed, follow the advice of Mackenzie, who says, "the yellow fever would effectually secure the island in case of an external attack if the policy of abandoning the coasts and destroying the towns were acted on." But will it not be far better not to put ourselves in a position where we must depend upon such dolorous auxilaries, or where municipal suicide would be the best of available defenses?

A TROPICAL CLIMATE NEVER EXEMPT FROM TROPICAL DISEASES.

There is a question of some gravity as to the salubrity of the climate in Santo Domingo. If it is really healthful why is it that its population has been forever on the wane? Its colored population, without thrift or fertility, steadily diminishes in number, and whites never go and stay there with any purpose to make it a family home. Concede that the soil is fertile and hot in its fecundity, then may it not be asked whether it is not true everywhere under a tropical sun that a country, rank to rottenness in its vegetation, is equally rank in its malarial diseases?

True, it would seem to cost nothing to raise children in Santo Domingo, because until they are five or six years old they go forth like our first parents in Paradise, without shame, as naked as they came into the world. Even adults are often content with little more than one garment, and are not very fastidious whether that is a shirt or a coat, a pair of pantaloons or a hat. Why is there no increase? In the first place, from universal and unconquerable indolence, no extensive crops are grown, and when any are grown the owners are in such constant dread of military raids and the periodical hurricanes, with both of which they are so often visited, as to make subsistence precarious. In the absence of these, droughts not unfrequently destroy large tracts of vegetation. A regular supply of food is necessary for any increase of population; and for this end tropical fruits, though ever so abundant in their season, are an insufficient substitute. But the hot seasons of every year are as fatal in their ravages as famine and epidemical diseases are sure to be active and vigorous, though the people are not. Malte Brun, speaking of the bay of Samana, says:

"The banks of that vast basin are unhealthy, and Europeans are unwilling to reside there."

Of course an excursion party, traveling on the bounty of the Government, with something of the pomp of Antony visiting Cleopatra, sped along by the imperial clarion of music, and leaving the stern frosts of a northern winter for the soft and sunny lap of the tropics, where the earth is all clad with greenest verdure, would be pleased and in smiles with everything; with the birds of the air, beasts of the field, and even with creeping things. They are happy. Severe and irreverent critics they cannot be. They are there for the purpose of being pleased; nobody expected anything less;

and they would be careful not to stay so long as to encounter the perils of the climate. How much knowledge, untinged by "the animated particles of the rainbow," would such an excursion party obtain as to the statistics of mortality in the fraction of five weeks of time, devoted to all the objects of their mission, not excluding social enjoyments and ceremonies, and, under the adroit manipulation of Baez, bankrupt, as he is in money, and with no reputation to spare? Birds of passage, even the wild geese, which go south in the winter and fly northward with the earliest breath of spring, might as well be summoned to testify about the dog-days they had never seen under the equator, as such a February party to testify touching the summer solstice at Santo Domingo.

The commissioners will be recognized as most intelligent and highly respected gentlemen, but their time was too short and their task too great. They will undoubtedly be able to state that tropical plants grow in tropical countries, and to refute all such stories as that related in the only joke ever perpetrated by Washington, as to Newark, that the mosquitoes are so fat and large as to "sting through the thickest boot;" but in the brief time they expended they must have been so hurried as to be obliged to follow in large measure the "memorandum for a tour" in New Jersey, to be found in Salmagundi, as follows:

"A knowing traveler always judges of everything by the inn-keepers and waiters—set down Newark people all as fat as butter—landlord member of the Legislature—treats everybody who has a vote—mem. all the inn-keepers members of Legislature of New Jersey—saw a large flock of crows—concluded there must be a dead horse in the neighborhood—mem. country remarkable for crows—won't let the horses die in peace."

Mr. President, I would take the word of the commissioners for £5,000, but I would not take their indorsement of the climate of Santo Domingo for more than five weeks.

But the fate of French and Spanish armies, early and late, disclose the facts. We know that, with the aid of the climate, a few ignorant, ill-clad, ill-fed, and ill armed Dominicans have destroyed large and well-appointed armies. Army statistics show what is the rate of mortality, when we compare the South with the North within the extreme limits of our own country, and these prove the mortality in the South to be nearly four times greater than in the North and East. The number constantly on the sick list from malarial fevers and dysentery is also vastly greater. Nobody will question that Jamaica is as healthy as Santo Domingo, and yet the average deaths there of the British army, from 1837 to 1855, were as great as at Bombay, or over sixty annually in every one thousand men, while in some years they reached the rate of three hundred men out of one thousand in a single year. This is a rate which destroys a whole regiment in about three years. In Canada the annual mortality is only reported at ten in one thousand men. It will thus be seen that military service in the West India Islands is more fatal to life than even that in Algeria, so much more destructive than the average home service to the French army. A change of the political sovereignty could hardly be expected to effect any change of the climate.

The colored race withstand the climate and the yellow fever somewhat better than the white race, but the bulk of our Army—three fourths at least—are recruited north of the Potomac, or from the cities of New York, Cincinnati, and Chicago, and are almost entirely white. At Key West we know the fearful fatality that attends our troops. It may be said that when sent to Santo Domingo they might be stationed in the interior, among the mountains, but there they would be useless, except in cases of insurrection. They must be placed on the coast and around harbors. These would be the places requiring defense, requiring a constant military police, and here our troops must lay their bones in obedience to laws they have no power to resist. Jamaica, Cuba, and Santo Domingo for years were called the graves of Europe. Do we want to make the latter the grave of America?

Eighty years ago there were twenty-three British forts in Jamaica, besides fourteen posts or batteries, with officers and men. How many there are now I know not, but probably there are not less. And how is that island held and governed now? Great Britain still holds the island, but its industry has perished, and she would probably be glad of an excuse to cut loose from it forever. Since the late rebellion there, resulting in such fearful tragedies, the entire authority is vested in the governor, assisted by a privy council, appointed by himself, consisting of six members, and a legislative council, consisting of the privy council and six non-official members. This shows conclusively that a West India government must be supported by an army, and also shows the arbitrary style of government which is still necessary after an occupancy of the island by the British ever since the time of Cromwell. Such men as Governor Eyre only can maintain order. It is also to be noted that when slavery existed there were, in a population of three hundred and forty thousand, thirty thousand whites, but in 1861 the whites were reduced to less than fourteen thousand. Is there not some proof in this that there is no health in the West India archipelago for white people? Who will say that Santo Domingo can be governed with less sacrifice of life or treasure than Jamaica? And Jamaica is much smaller than Santo Domingo.

The history of Santo Domingo, early and late, shows the climate to be incompatible with labor. It is a sad reflection that its million or more of native inhabitants, when reduced to forced labor, were all speedily exterminated. From the highest numbers, whatever those may have been, only sixty thousand were left in the short space of fifteen years, and in forty-years no more than two hundred of the original inhabitants remained. When their places were filled, from time to time, by millions more of other Indians and hardier sons of Africa, even these stubborn races gave way, and for two centuries the climate appears to have been most destructive to the vitality of the human race, drawn from whatever quarter of the globe.

The experiments made within the last five years show that of some hundreds of men hired to go and work on Santo Domingo plantations nearly all were stricken down by disease, and few lived to return. The woeful mortality which followed more than four hundred freedmen, an enterprise for a time in charge of the Senator from Kansas, [Mr. POMEROY,] landed at Isle à Vache, Hayti, and from which our Government had to rescue the survivors at great expense and scandal, is too notorious to be disputed.

Mr. POMEROY. As there can be no discussion on this subject after the Senator concludes, I hope he will not connect me with any such scheme as that. I had no more to do with it than a dead man.

Mr. MORRILL, of Vermont. The Senator from Kansas had charge of the $500,000 raised for the purpore of colonizing some freedmen.

Mr. POMEROY. But I say, as to those who went to Hayti, I had no more to do with it than a dead man, and protested against them all the time.

Mr. MORRILL, of Vermont. It was not my purpose to impute any blame to the Senator. One chapter of the historian, Alison, I think I have shown to be a chapter of blunders, and I shall now turn over another leaf and quote from a passage on the West India islands, where he is sustained by all standard authorities, and where he is most probably entirely right. He says:

> "It is a land of slavery and pestilence, where indolence dissolves the manly character and stripes can alone arouse the languid arm; where death bestrides the evening gale, and the yielding breath inhales poison with its delight; where the iron race of Japhet itself seems melting away under the prodigality of the gifts of nature."

This is the salubrity to which we are so earnestly invited! It appears to me the less we have of it the better.

From the report on commercial relations (Executive Document No. 18) transmitted to the House of Representatives December 5, 1870, by the Secretary of State, I find valuable information communicated by our commercial agent, J. Somers Smith, at Santo Domingo, which fully corroborates the statements already given as to the utter poverty of the resources of the country and its extreme unhealthfulness. The whole document shows that while sugar cane is grown it is consumed in its crude state or converted into molasses and rum. Coffee may be grown, but not enough is produced for their own consumption, and it is imported and sold at retail for twenty-five cents, gold. Nothing considerable is produced except tobacco. They are dependent on the United States for even potatoes, onions, beets, flour, butter, lard, and cheese. They have some mahogany, but there is no demand for it. I will ask the Secretary to read from the document as I have marked on page 338.

The Chief Clerk read as follows:

> "Cotton and cocoa are raised in insignificant quantities. There are no productions from mines in Santo Domingo. The exaggerated accounts published in the United States are gotten up by adventurers who have obtained concessions for nothing and expect to realize profits from the credulity of their fellow-citizens. There is no question that there are indications of copper and gold, as these metals have been found in small quantities, but it is extremely doubtful whether enterprises in search of these hidden riches would be profitable. As a warning to such as may be tempted to embark capital in Dominican mining enterprises, it is proper to state that Mr. Heneken, an English gentleman who resided in this country more than thirty years, was constantly engaged in visiting all parts of the island. He was a member of the Geological Society of London, and employed scientific engineers and Cornish miners, but it proved to be labor lost. He died about five years ago, impoverished and disappointed. The wealth of this country consists in its various cabinet, lignum-vitæ, and dye-woods, and the fertility of its soil, which is capable of producing all tropical plants in abundance; but it languishes in consequence of its constant revolutionary state, and because it has but a small and ignorant population. Efforts have been made at times to introduce a white immigration, but unsuccessfully. Nearly all the immigrants from Europe and the United States fell victims to the climate in a very short time after their arrival. This fact is repeatedly recorded in the ard chives of this consulate. There are no white field-laborers in Santo Domingo."

Mr. MORRILL, of Vermont. I present this report of an authorized agent of our Government, resident of Santo Domingo, and sent to Congress by the Secretary of State, as a very satisfactory document to be read and hung up alongside of the report of our late commissioners; but I must say that I have no idea that our commercial agent, by anticipation, intended to refer to any "exaggerated accounts" published by the commission.

BAEZ WANTS THE MORAL FORCE OF GUNS—HIS PEOPLE MAY PREFER THE UNITED STATES TO BAEZ.

But were all other circumstances as favorable to Dominican annexation as they are in fact repugnant to the scheme, there still remains one more vital consideration, namely, do the people of Santo Domingo really desire to sink their independent existence and be permanently stitched to the mere selvage of the United States? Decidedly no! The ruling passion of the people, mainly descendants of Indians and forty different African races, is a hatred of the white race. Smothered it may be for a time, but it is sure sooner or later to crop out. In the Haytien part of the island, where the same races prevail, white persons are excluded from becoming citizens and from becoming owners of land. They have really sought independence, and have abundant faith in their own autonomy, if they could only keep the Haytiens at bay. The fact is conceded by the commissioners that they would now prefer independence if they believed that to be possible.

A temporary gust may now blow in favor of the United States; they may want to realize the $600,000 to pay off back salaries; they may fear Baez while he seems to carry already the United States flag; they may yearn for peace so that they will not be conscripted to fight in the army of Baez; they may only echo opinions of leaders to day which they will be ready to change to-morrow; they may expect sudden wealth and not taxation; but it would be a great mistake to suppose that Dominicans have more respect or affection for the United States than they have for France or Spain. From language, religion, and association their inhering partialities must all be in favor of the Latin race and the infallible Catholic church.

In 1848 the present adventurer, Baez, attempted to sell out his country to France. In 1861, not to load the recital with other instances, Santana made a transfer of Domingo to Spain, at the time with universal applause. But very soon the people were inspired with other sentiments, and would not submit. Within three years they drove all the Spanish forces out of their territory, and Spain, with enormous losses, once more abandoned Santo Domingo. There is no more reason to suppose the people favor the annexation now proposed than that which they then trampled in the dust of a revolution. The rival chiefs, whose baseness is only equaled by their pride, and whose treachery is surpassed only by their servility, may seek safety, titles, and wealth by such a measure; but the people, whatever they or others may now say or think, will ever stand ready to accept the lead of any patriotic chief who may hereafter raise, however rudely, the banner of revolt or of independence.

Already evidence is accumulating which shows the popular vote, obtained through the enticements of Baez and the moral force of the guns of the United States Navy, to have been a delusive juggle. A vote so swift and so one-sided affords grounds for suspicion, especially when the imprisonment of the first negative voter disclosed the compulsatory part of the process. The banishment or imprisonment of those known to be opposed to annexation is also an ugly feature. Cabral, not inferior in cunning nor in popular favor to Baez, declares the popular vote in favor of annexation "a sham." Cabral, and fighting men enough to frighten if not to overwhelm Baez, whenever the stars and stripes and the "moral support" of our guns, as our Secretary of the Navy softly calls it, shall be withdrawn, Cabral and his party protest against the validity of the whole transaction, are now in arms successfuly disputing it, and the popular vote seems to have been a poor copy of the very poorest Napoleonism. It is clear that Santo Domingo could only be held by a military and naval force, as it has been held for the past year by our Navy. The masses, however confused and unstable upon other matters, have a traditional aversion to the rule of any foreign nation, manifested in their public records, and on many bloody fields of battle, which it would be sheer blindness to disregard.

It should be borne in mind also that the consent of Hayti seems to be as essential to the transfer of territory as that of Santo Domingo itself. Without such consent even now border warfare seems breaking forth from every jungle and which Baez is incompetent to grapple with, but piteously asks the United States for aid to suppress. Cabral and Luperon, and their malcontents, with the aid of the dusky warriors of Hayti, always ready for an unrelenting crusade against the whites, might prove a formidable foe in a desperate climate even to the United States.

It should also be noted that of the 22,212 square miles now claimed by Santo Domingo 1,000 square miles are reported to be held and occupied by Cabral or by Hayti. Did the commissioners penetrate this part of the island? But suppose it were to be admitted that every Dominican, those who have large claims for unpaid salaries and those who expect salaries hereafter, as well as those who hold leases of land in expectation of annexation, was known to be in favor of the measure, would that be any reason why we should be? It might be a very good bargain for them and yet a very bad one for us. Are we to accept of all peoples and tribes who may express a desire for such a union? A patrimony quite ample, if properly husbanded, by such a course would soon be squandered.

Finally, no Dominican can be legally bound by any compact which carries with it territorial sovereignty. Their latest constitution declares that "neither the whole nor any part of the territory shall be alienated." We know, therefore, that not even the conscience of Baez, nor that of any other Dominican, can be in the way of repudiating an act so manifestly illegal and constitutionally indefensible.

It will be seen that I place little reliance upon any evidence that the Dominican people are largely in favor of being annexed to the United States. If the assertion be made that fifty or more Americans would be sufficient to mold and shape the destinies of the whole of Santo Domingo, it should be remembered that a greater number of Americans have been hovering in and about the island for more than a year and a half. Doubtless they have not been wholly without influence; but the disinterested government of Baez, whose salary, and that of all his cabinet, legislature, and judiciary, will be likely to remain unpaid unless annexation succeeds, has staked its existence upon the success of the scheme. Hence the anxiety for success, without which they must fight for the doubtful honor of supremacy in the administration of the Government. There is an exigency which requires foreign aid to relieve. That may be the opinion of the entire party of Baez. I do not think the United States Government ought to be used for his extrication.

THE PUBLIC VOICE AGAINST THE MEASURE.

I have admired the President's inflexible perseverance more than his political sagacity in adhering to the policy of Dominican annexation in the face of undeniable evidence that there was no sentiment in the country of any party or of any State warmly in its favor, because it brings to mind his inflexibility in braver and grander enterprises, and I have no doubt of his patriotic motives. The House of Representatives, by a vote of nearly two to one, have once pronounced against it. On the 1st of February, 1869, a resolution giving the assent of Congress to the project of annexation was defeated by a vote of 110 against 62. The non-committal amendment to the joint resolution authorizing the expedition to Santo Domingo was a hostile one, and it was carried in the House of Representatives by thirty majority, and I am assured that the naked question of annexation would have been defeated by a still larger majority. In the present House of Representatives it is likely to receive a more decided rebuff; and yet a vote of the House will be necessary, or the appropriation to carry the measure into effect will fail. The Senate, as we learn from the message, has rejected a treaty of annexation. All this should be counted conclusive as to the unbiased opinion of the highest legislative bodies of the country, and most likely as fairly reflecting the sentiments of the people. Opinions of any other sort can be put off as cheaply as put on, and it would not be complimentary to the national Legislature to suppose they would act on any other.

The treaty of annexation itself awakened no enthusiasm, and was smothered by cold neglect and by an almost universal silence. So improbable seemed its success that it was not even dignified by denunciation. But upon a measure of so much gravity ought not the people to be heard from before the question is settled forever? Let the people, at least, have time to consider whether they could afford to accept any part or the whole of the island even as a gift; much more, whether they can afford to buy it at any price, or at the cost of war. If it is the first step in a policy of diseased enlargement, which any lover of his country might look upon with the gravest apprehension, there should be some opportunity left for escape.

The annexation of Santo Domingo would be the extension of empire unaccompanied by any addition to the empire of national stability and virtue. Our territory is already enormous, and every map, through constant additions and new explorations, becomes annually antiquated and as useless as a gray-haired almanac. We should build our Republic to last, and not for the show of a single season. When Alexander retreated from India he caused to be made and scattered arms much larger than his men could use, and higher mangers and heaver bits than were suitable for his horses, to impress foreign nations with an exaggerated idea of his greatness. But this trick of the showman is now only remembered as a folly. We shall fail to impress the world by playing the giant abroad and the pigmy at home, or by spreading great American flags abroad while those at home, torn and tattered, fail to command respect and obedience, or by sending our symbols of power where they will be surrounded, not only by a Babylonian confusion of languages, but where we can have no directing and constructive power over the character of the people. To be strong we must have the love of a thoroughly amalgamated people, and something more than mere local patriotism. Real strength does not consist so much in power to conquer the world as in power to resist the world, and even wealth is much less often found by going abroad after new objects than by search at home for and diligent use of such as we already possess. We may also virtually extend our territory by extending our knowledge of that we now have, and cultivating its present resources, its natural affinities, and its future possibilities. The glory of a State does not consist merely in the magnitude of its extent, but largely in a fit correspondence of all its parts and the mutual respect and habitual affection of its people.

SANTO DOMINGO AND HER DEBTS GO TOGETHER.

No one can doubt if the late treaty had been ratified, or if annexation should at last succeed, that the United States, having diverted the little remnants of what it is a farce to call the national property of Santo Domingo, having shielded her by absorption from responsibility to other nations as well as to individuals for debts, and having appropriated all her resources from customs duties, would be bound, by international law as well as by honor, to pay all of her outstanding obligations, whatever the amount, however contracted, and under whatever administration. No stipulation between ourselves and Baez to the contrary, if made, would have any more lasting force than that made with Texas, or would bind other parties, or be worth the paper upon which it might be written. A State or Territory cannot be prosecuted for debt like an individual. The United States itself would resist any such indignity, and would be held to account for the old scores of any territory annexed as surely as the husband, if the wife be indebted before marriage, is bound afterward to pay the debt, having adopted her and her circumstances together; and this Dominican debt nominally amounts to millions, as it has been contracted upon a depreciated credit and a depreciated currency, itself a debt yet to be redeemed. The creditors are widely scattered, and some are citizens of nations who will protect their rights to the last extremity.

Many of these debts may be questionable; but the proof of their validity, supported by interested swearers, would be impregnable. There are many large unsettled war claims which cannot even be estimated. Hayti announces a very large claim, by no means easily to be settled. One administration acknowledges one class of claims and another a different class. Who is to decide? Is it not absurd for the present Dominican Government to give a schedule of their debts, which is reduced by their own illegal and arbitrary edicts from four hundred to one, from sixty to one, from thirty to one, and from one third to one sixth? Will their creditors abide such scaling? It is wholly improbable; and yet it is solely by this process and by omitting all account of interest they have contracted to pay, and which is overdue, that they are able to compress their debt within the prescribed limits of $1,500,000. Instead of $1,500,000 in gold, the whole debt is quite likely to be very much more, how much no one can tell. Ratify such a treaty and the bottom of Dominican claims would not be sounded in the present generation, but a fresh brood of claim agents, like carrion birds, would flock to the Capitol for their prey. Our action in the case of Texas is not likely to be forgotten. The joint resolution in that case, March 1, 1845, roundly and stoutly provided:

"That Texas should retain all her public lands, debts, taxes, and dues of every kind, and all vacant and unappropriated lands, to be applied to the payment of the debts and liabilities of said republic of Texas, and the residue of said lands, after discharging said debts and liabilities, to be disposed of as said State may direct, *but in no event are said debts and liabilities to become a charge upon the Government of the United States.*"

And yet, when the clamorous Slidell and others had become the holders of these claims to a large amount, on the 9th of September, 1855, all claim upon the United States for liability was once more relinquished, and Congress paid to the State of Texas in bonds the sum of $10,000,000; but Texas was not even trusted to pay these greedy creditors herself, as they were adroitly required to give receipts to the United States themselves for not less than $5,000,000, or their share of the job. Is there not something like this looming up in Dominica? Will not her creditors say, as Ruth said to Naomi, "Entreat me not to leave thee, or to return from following after thee, for whither thou goest I will go."

THE AMERICAN CHARACTER WORTH PRESERVING.

The people of the United States have some pride as to their character—personal and national—that which they inherited and that which they have made for themselves. They claim that all men were born equal, but they do not claim that all have equally improved the talents given to them by the great Father of all mankind. They claim, and justly, that self-government is the best of all governments; not that all men can or will govern themselves, nor that it can be safely intrusted to the untrained, unlettered people of many other nations. Is Santo Domingo one of the transcendent exceptions? Not at all; and we know that its incorporation under our flag would be the incorporation of an inferior element, designed to invite much larger accessions of the same sort; and as such a precursor it may be encouraged by those who would like nothing so much as to chronicle republican degradation, though themselves not unwilling to be released from such far-off dependencies. To-day Great Britain does not regard Gibraltar, Quebec, or Malta as essential to British power. Of what use is Gibraltar as against Russia or Prussia? Great Britain cannot suppose the United States are afraid of Quebec. She is conscious that her North American provinces, though inhabited by a gallant people, could not be held in time of war for a single month as against its more powerful neighbors, and knows equally well that, in like circumstances, she could terminate any hold we might have on Santo Domingo in a much shorter time. Fortified places count very little in the presence of a vigorous enemy. The engineers of destruction nearly always prove more potent than the engineers of defense.

Annexation of any sort, if to be accepted by us—and there is no possible annexation which would not be more profitable to the party annexed than to ourselves—should seek us, and ought not to be bought, conquered, or obtained by any of the common acts of diplomacy. It should come, spotless as a prairie homestead, as a free-will offering of lands, hands, and hearts, and not be too eagerly sought, as though a few acres of the nether regions were indispensable to our paradise. Were all Spain to be offered to us to-day on the same terms proposed by Baez for Santo Domingo it would, of course, be instantly declined, and yet its incorporation into our system presents less insuperable objections; the people are much more intelligent; but larger numbers, by magnifying the enormity, only make the ugly features of such a proposition more visible.

The United States should have too much

self-respect to accept of any annexation save such as would add political and moral strength to her free institutions, wisdom to her councils, and buttresses to her Constitution, and cannot afford to favor, nor can President Grant with his grand history afford to favor, the annexation of a people, confessedly inferior to the French, or to the Spanish, or to any other European nationality, whose latest constitution forbids the alienation of their soil, and whose present chief is confessedly too weak to maintain ascendency over his own countrymen except through the standing menace of the flag and guns of the United States Navy. It will touch our honor if it shall turn out that we hold up a chief in order to make or to hold up a treaty. We may even make some of the ancient British acquisitions of Lord Clive and Warren Hastings in India respectable by such a modern indorsement.

I cannot but regard a policy, though it be only the first step in the direction of what may be called tropical annexation, which would tend to make our nation a conglomerate of different habitudes and nationalities, instead of one united, compact whole, as fraught with unmistakable calamities. An empire may be able, through its more despotic rule, for a time to hold discordant peoples in subjection; but make such materials sovereign and equal, as we must—for we accept for ourselves nothing less, crowning all with our fourteenth and fifteenth amendments—and it would be only a question of time as to how soon they would, by introducing extravagance, corruption, local divisions and collisions, wreck the best form of constitutional government ever devised by the wit of man and ruin the fairest hope of the world.

THE WARNINGS OF HISTORY.

Unfortunately, the life of republics has not been immortal. There is one, however, that has stood unchanged fourteen hundred years amid all surrounding changes; but San Marino is not only the oldest but the smallest State in Europe, a State that never courted destruction by expansion.

The lessons of history, I am aware, are litte heeded, and a fast people in a headlong pursuit of material interests often refuse to recognize that they are on the same road marked by the bleached skeletons of nations wasted or fatally stricken down by the results of a similar mad ambition. Conceding that the despotism which controls an empire may be the best adapted among all governmental institutions for the control of colonies, distant provinces, and foreign territories, let us see how it has fared with a few of such examples in the past, and where success might be looked for, if anywhere.

Alexander pursued territorial acquisitions until tradition records that he wept because he could no longer find a new world to conquer, having acquired in seven years an empire as large as that acquired by the Romans in seven hundred; but the great Alexander was no sooner dead than his colossal empire was found to be as incurably debauched as he was known to have been himself, and the empire was at once broken into numerous military fragments to vex the world with new wars and a fresh brood of tyrants. At last Macedonia itself, the ancient seat of Philip and the base of the son's power, was reduced to a mere Roman province, while the city of Alexandria, built to perpetuate the name and splendor of its founder, has long been a conquest under the dominion of the Turks, who give away its ruins, with barbaric munificence, to British museums.

The decline and fall of Rome was made certain when it commenced its work of centuries of triumphant and ferocious territorial aggrandizement. In his last will the advice of Augustus against this policy came too late. The blunder he would restrain had already been committed. The people of vast untutored provinces were made Roman citizens, but these foreign-made citizens only served to undermine the power and glory of the original seat of Roman greatness, which diminished in its stamina and virtue—the main pillars of any State—as rapidly as it increased in its bulk of gross material possessions. Gibbon asserts and abundantly proves that the Roman people were dissolved into the common mass and confounded with millions of inferior provincials. The institutions of Rome were destroyed by the poison everywhere lurking in and around ill-advised territorial expansions. Even the exalted type of ancient Roman virtue and manhood was unequal to the strain, and the country of the Scipios and Cæsars was finally vanquished, and vanquished by even the Huns—even as Egypt was conquered and for centuries ruled by the Mamalukes. So much for ancient examples. Let us now come down to a later period of history, without even glancing at the rapid decadence of Mohammedan conquests, and watch the inflexible result.

Spain under Charles II became the proudest nation of the earth, in consequence of the extent and importance of its territorial acquisitions, both in the Old World and the new. She could boast of Castile, Aragon, and Navarre, of Milan, Naples, Sicily, and Sardinia, of Cape Verd and the Canaries, of Tunis, of the Philippines and the Moluccas, of Peru, Chili, and Mexico, and finally, under Charles V, of Cuba and Hispaniola; and it is a part of this last ill-omened island which our excellent President has so earnestly sought to clutch. But all of these more or less magnificent Spanish appendages contributed only a momentary splendor to Spain, and then for the most part they dropped from the parent stem like overripe fruit, and brought a deeper and more lasting humiliation upon that haughty but exhausted country than has been visited upon any other nation in modern times. The riches from the tributes of enslaved peoples, succeeded by luxury and effeminacy, proved to be apples that turned to ashes in the mouth.

Take the case of Bonaparte, who would have made, to borrow the language of one of our best American thinkers, "the earth for his pasture and the sea for his pond," and where are his possessions now? The ode of Byron fitly answers:

"Is this the man of thousand thrones,
Who strew'd our earth with hostile bones?
And can he thus survive?
Since he, miscall'd the morning star,
Nor man nor fiend hath fallen so far."

And these words almost as well apply to Napoleon the last as to the first.

There is, however, still another recent example. I mean that of the famous house of Hapsburg, or the emperor of Austria, who recently, besides Germans, held under his command Italians, Poles, Croats, Dalmatians, Slovaks, Romans and Hungarians; but the battle of Sadowa left Francis Joseph among the poorest and saddest monarchs of Europe, and from the first rank, Austria, cut in twain by the astute and relentless Bismark, fell to a second-rate position among the nations of the earth, henceforth with ample leisure to reflect upon the hollowness and folly of incongruous annexations under one dominion of separate, remote, and diverse peoples.

Are we to shut our eyes to such significant facts, which stand forth, as light-houses upon dangerous coasts, in all the pages of history? Can any one be under the delusion that human nature has greatly changed or that the United States are to have a charmed life and be exempt from all perils however recklessly guided? It appears to me that these great historic facts should have their proper influence—and I ask no more—in the decision of the question before us. Shall we not first of all preserve the inheritance of our fathers?

It may be said that England has not endangered its permanence, or its solid foundations, by its extensive colonial system. That remains yet to be solved. Her mastery has been maintained at the immense cost of her present national debt and her present and past system of taxation, and of such a navy as makes it not inappropriate for her poets to boast that "Britannia rules the waves;" but it must be borne in mind that no British colony is represented, or has any control, in the home government. British statesmen are not embarrassed by any such foreign admixture. Australia, New Zealand, India, and the African and North American colonies may not forever submit to imperial control, nor will their separation from it be likely to be restrained by force. At present the British empire in India stands firmly—bating rather too frequent mutinies and revolts—but are there not eruptive social and political symptoms at home which at present tax all the resources of the most consummate British statesmanship? Even Gladstone's constituents petition him to resign because he has made them paupers. In the event of internal commotion, or of a great war, Great Britain has no colony which could take her part or that would contribute a penny to her exchequer or a man to her army. Charles XII said he taught his enemies how to conquer him, and it may be found that the British will have taught the Irish, as well as the Indian Sepoys, an art which may hereafter plague even British conquerors. At any rate, it is apparent that Russia, Denmark, and Spain, as well as England, no longer cling to colonies with their ancient tenacity. They can part with them without any heart-breaking.

The framers and founders of our Government seem to have been diligent students of history, and the debates in the constitutional Convention, as well as the papers composing the Federalist, show that they were keenly alive to all the facts bearing upon the career and fate of republican forms of government. Under the old Confederation a union of Canada and other British provinces with the United States was openly contemplated and provided for, but when the Constitution of 1789 was ordained and established such a union had become apparently hopeless, and the expatriated Tories having made the provinces their home, it was then undesirable, and perhaps repugnant to the ardent patriotism of the States. At all events, the peril which tracks the unlimited extension of territory in the progress of nations in all ages of the world was so obvious and so grave in its character that no power was anywhere given, under our Constitution, by which such acquisitions were to be ever authorized, directly or indirectly. In other words, they were all forever soberly and silently renounced.

This should be a barrier high enough at least to make us pause before we attempt to leap over it. It is not enough that the plain and palpable force of the Constitution has been disregarded; ought it to be again and now? The advantages should be overwhelmingly in favor of any scheme of annexation before it should be even mooted, and its character such as would be cordially approved by the people of all sections and of all parties of our country. Nothing less can justify any annexation. It should not be a doubtful question carried by a beggarly and reluctant vote. Can it be doubted, if ever carried at all, it must be by hesitating votes and by the leanest of constitutional numbers, whether by treaty or the legerdemain of a joint resolution? Can it be doubted that the annexation of Santo Domingo, with the long, dark train which drags just in the rear, would have been rejected with scorn by the wise founders of our Government? Certainly it has no element of character and no advantage of position which can contribute to the safety or glory of our peerless Republic. All history shows that we ought to beware of what could not be other than a hot-bed for the germination of national discord, national extravagance, and national effeminacy.

It will not be pretended that there has been any enlightened public judgment in favor of the annexation of Santo Domingo. There has been all that in favor of President Grant; and his well-earned popularity, in spite of his Dominicanism, constitutes the entire strength, the back-bone of the measure. Unindorsed by him, may I not venture to say it would not have had or have a corporal's guard of supporters? To me, as well as to some others, it would have given peculiar pleasure to have been able to support the measure because of the countenance lent to it by the present Administration, of whose integrity of purpose I have not a shadow of doubt; but it was and is a question in its scope beyond the life of any party and far above all parties, and my responsibility began at the point where that of the Executive most properly leaves off; and if I could not independently and conscientiously acquit myself of my whole duty on a question which so profoundly concerns the destiny of our country, and, which once decided in the affirmative, is irrevocable, I should hold myself unworthy of my place. My age, if not my experience, warns me to endeavor to be earnestly for the right. The question and the measure of responsibility for its decision invoke the largest patriotism.

Individuals occupy but a brief space in the march of time, and a generation blots them out, perhaps forever, but nations have a continuity lasting for ages and a character to be transmitted to the immortal pages of future history. The past of our country is secure, and I would not jeopardize the future by the empty mockery of an exchange of moral grandeur for apparent or even for *real* material greatness. If I can divine the secrets of my own heart—and what I claim for myself I cordially concede to others—there is no passion, no sentiment lurking there which does not bow to a profound desire that our country should stand foremost among the nations of the earth, foremost in free and liberal institutions, foremost in its moral fiber and intellectual reach, foremost in literature, arts, and laws, and foremost in all the glories which crown the most elevated civilization and the most liberal, and, I hope I may add, stable form of human government.

But, regarding the annexation of Dominica in all its aspects, present and future, foreign and domestic, as boding no good to our country, as a policy withering to its highest and noblest aspirations, and as at war with the

"Unity and married calm of States,"

which all of us should most diligently seek, I shall vote against any measure even squinting at such an annexation, should such ever again come up, with a solemn and abiding conviction that I shall never have an opportunity of tendering to my country a higher service.

www.ingramcontent.com/pod-product-compliance
Lightning Source LLC
LaVergne TN
LVHW011140110826
845150LV00008B/2437
* 9 7 8 1 4 1 8 1 9 3 1 5 7 *